Volume 7

easy
GUITAR
play along

Audio Access Included

PLAYBACK+
Speed • Pitch • Balance • Loop

BLUES
SONGS FOR BEGINNERS
PLAY 8 SONGS WITH TAB AND SOUND-ALIKE AUDIO

T0079559

To access audio visit:
www.halleonard.com/mylibrary

Enter Code
3485-1754-9506-3776

ISBN 978-1-4768-1757-6

HAL•LEONARD®
7777 W. BLUEMOUND RD. P.O. BOX 13819 MILWAUKEE, WI 53213

Bright Lights, Big City

Words and Music by Jimmy Reed

cit - y, they've gone to my ba - by's head. ___ I ___ tried ___

4th time, To Coda $\oplus$

___ to tell the wom-an, but she don't be-lieve a word I said. ___

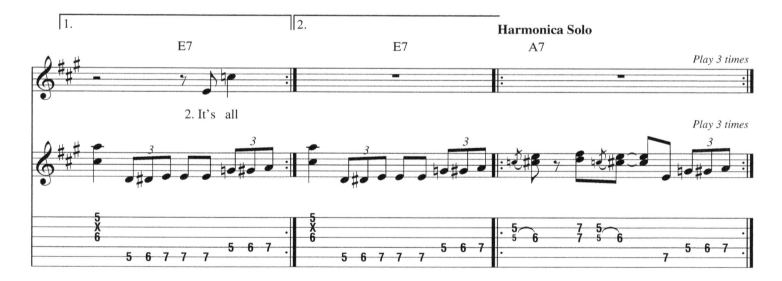

Harmonica Solo

2. It's all

Play 3 times

Play 3 times

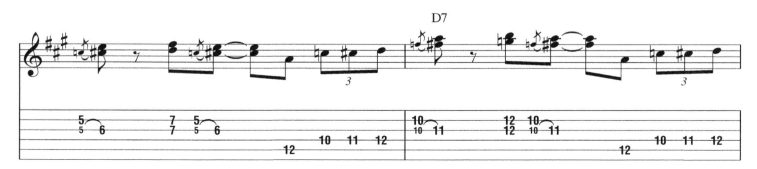

Additional Lyrics

2. It's all right, pretty baby, gonna need my help someday, you will.
   It's all right, pretty baby, you're gonna need my help someday, you will.
   You're gonna wish you had, a, listened to some of those things I said.

3. Go ahead, pretty baby, honey, knock yourself out.
   Oh, go ahead, pretty baby, honey, knock yourself out.
   I still love you baby, 'cause you don't know what it's all about.

4. The bright lights, the big city, they went to my baby's head.
   Oh, the bright lights, the big city, they went to my baby's head.
   I hope you remember, a, some of those things I said.

Double Trouble

Words and Music by Otis Rush

Intro
Moderately ♩ = 70

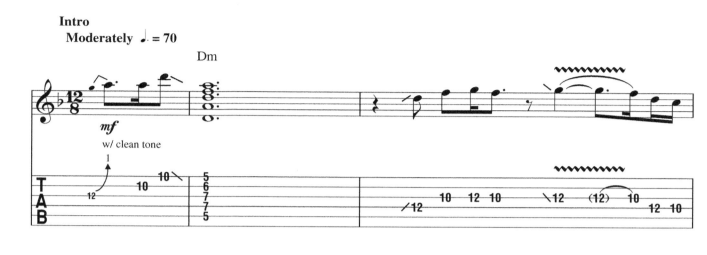

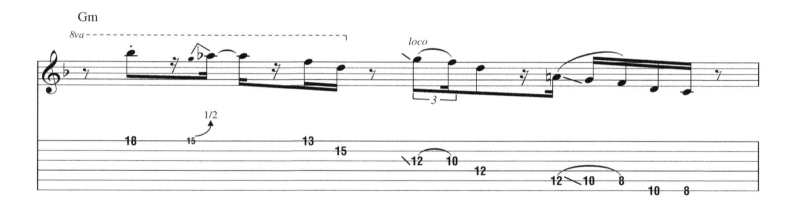

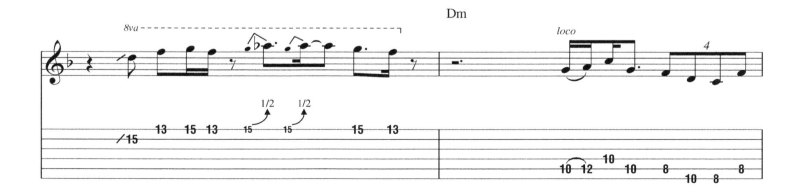

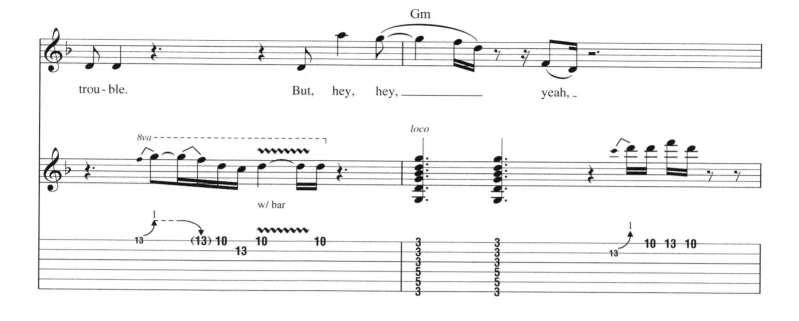

trou - ble.   But, hey, hey, _____ yeah, _

they say you can make _ it   if you try.

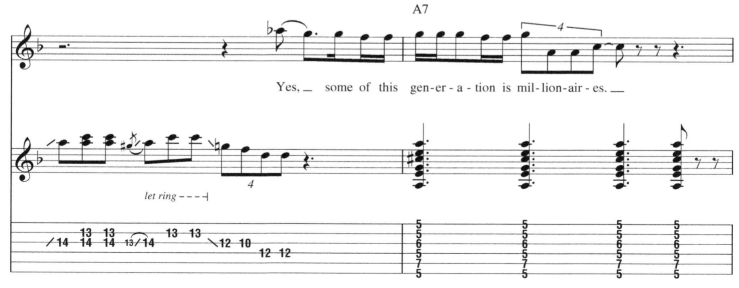

Yes, _ some of this gen - er - a - tion is mil - lion - air - es. _

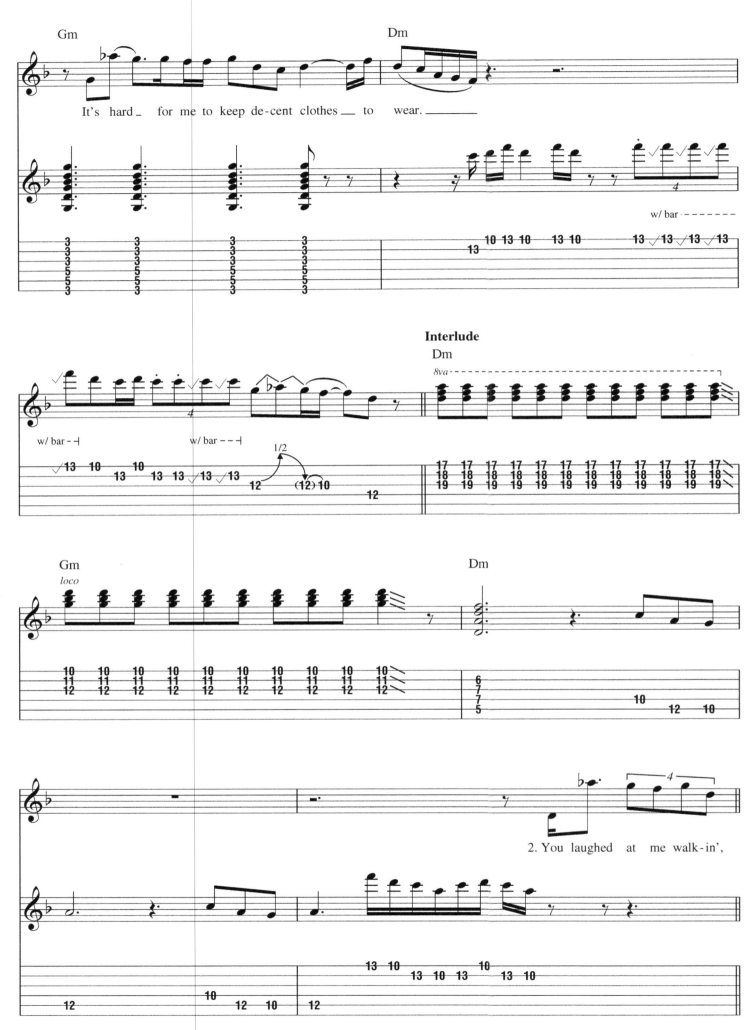

It's hard _ for me to keep de-cent clothes _ to wear. _

Interlude

2. You laughed at me walk-in',

Verse

ba - by, when I had ___ no ___ place _ to go.

Bad luck and trou - ble tak - en me, ___ I have no mon - ey to show. _

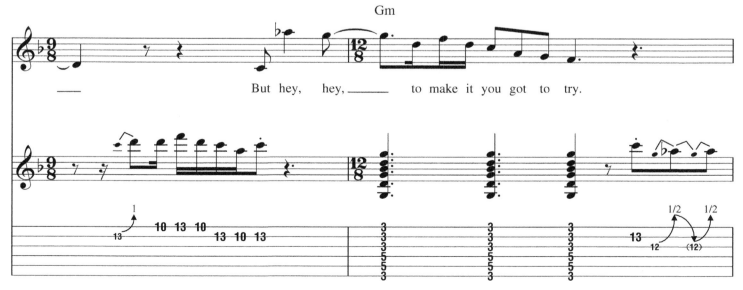

But hey, hey, ___ to make it you got to try.

9

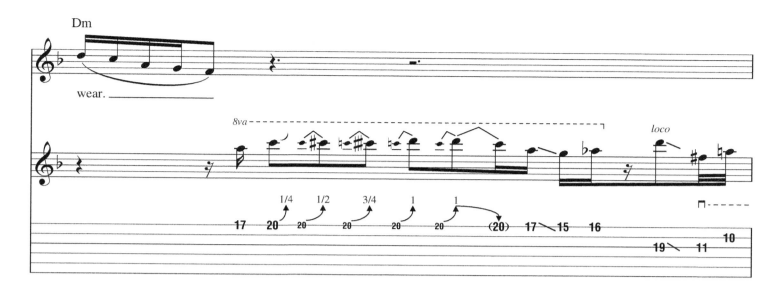

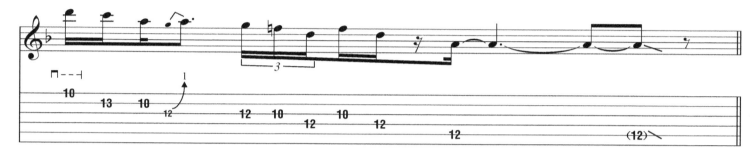

Outro

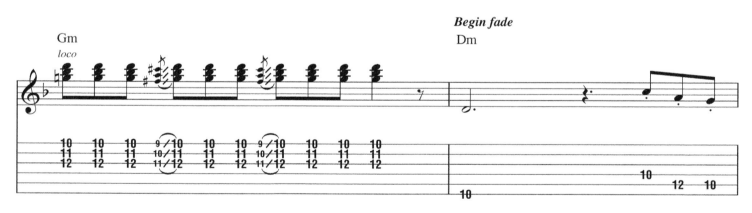

Begin fade

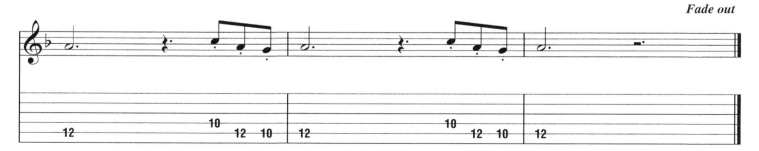

Fade out

Gangster of Love

Words and Music by Johnny Watson

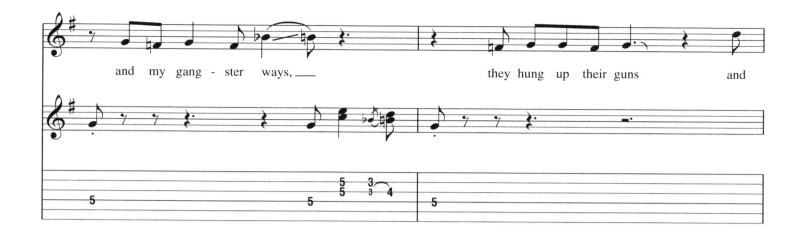

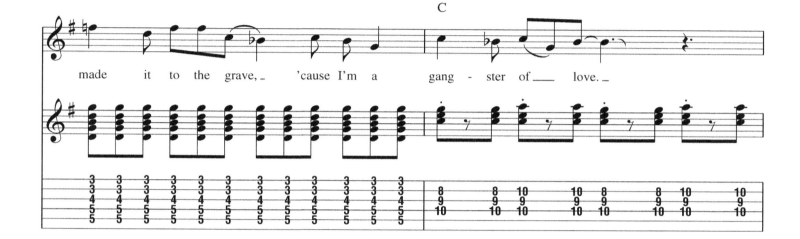

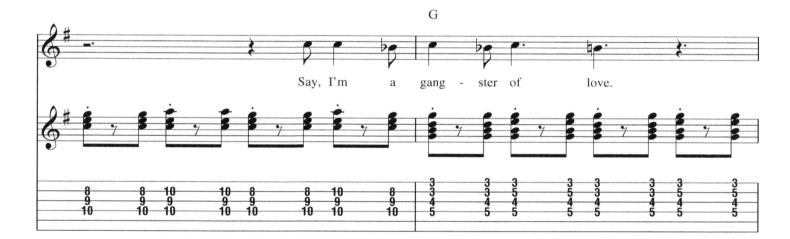

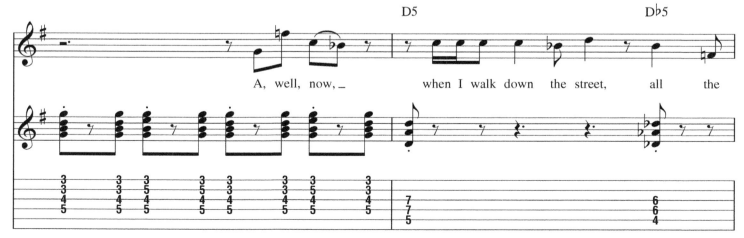

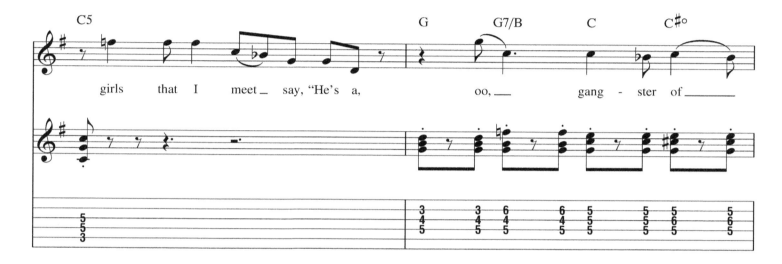

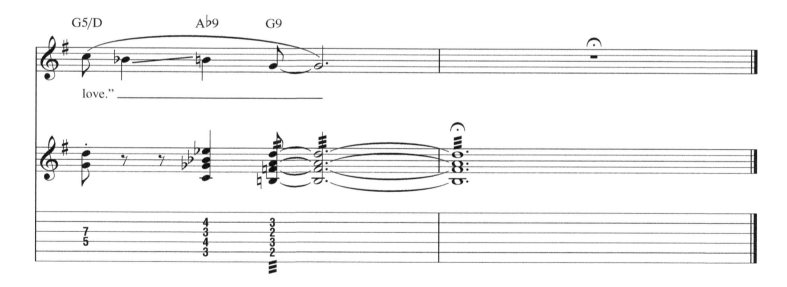

Additional Lyrics

2. I robbed a local beauty contest for their first place winner.
   They found her with me out in Hollywood, eatin' a big steak dinner.
   They tried to get her to go back to pick up her prize.
   She stood up and told them, "You just don't realize that he's a gangster of love."
   Early in the mornin', gangster of love. Oo, yeah, now.
   When I walk in a bar, girls from, from near and far say, "He's a gangster of love."

I'm Ready

Written by Willie Dixon

read - y as an - y - bod - y can be.   I am

read - y for you. ___   I hope   you ___ read - y for me.

%· Verse

2. I got an   axe - han - dled pis - tol on a   grave - yard frame. ___   Shoot - in'
3., 4. *See additional lyrics*

tomb - stone bul - lets, wear - in'   balls   and chain. I'm drink - in'   T.   N.   T.   I'm smok - in'

dy - na - mite. __ I hope some screw-ball __ start a fight __ 'cause I'm

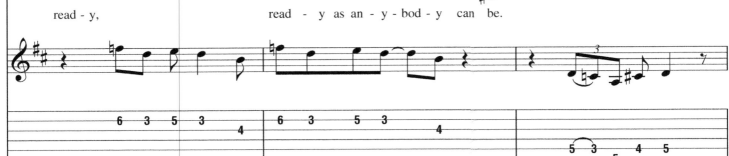

read - y, read - y as an - y - bod - y can be.

I am read - y for you. __ I hope you __ read - y for me.

Fill 1

Well, al - right.

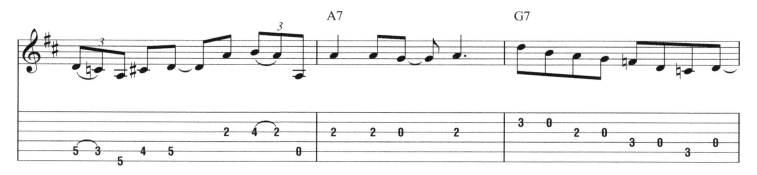

Additional Lyrics

3. All you pretty little chicks with your curly hair,
   I know you feel like I ain't nowhere.
   But stop what you're doin', baby, come over here.
   I'll prove to you, baby, that I ain't no square,
   Because I'm ready, ready as anybody can be.
   I am ready for you. I hope you ready for me.
   You hear me? You hear me?

4. I been drinkin' gin like never before.
   I feel so good that I want you to know.
   One more drink; I wish you would.
   It takes a whole lot of lovin' to make me feel good.
   Well, I'm ready, ready as anybody can be.
   I am ready for you. I hope you ready for me.

Let Me Love You Baby

Words and Music by Willie Dixon

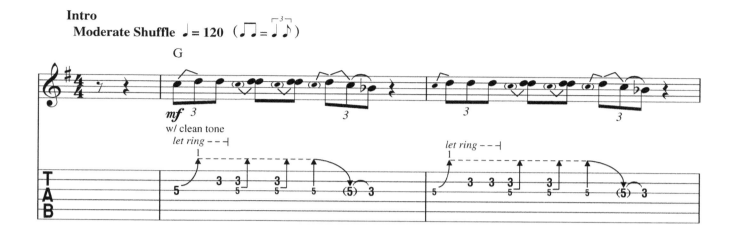

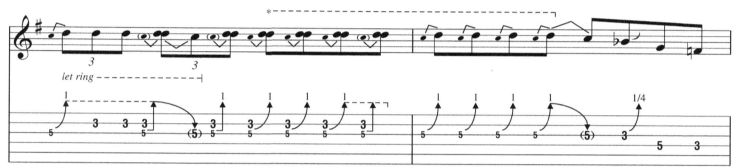

*Played as even eighth notes.

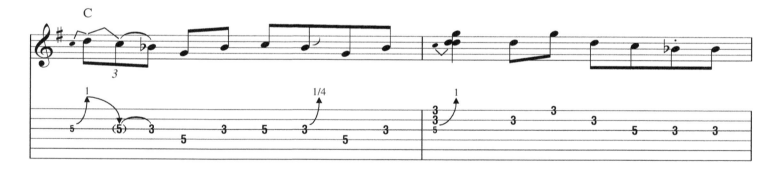

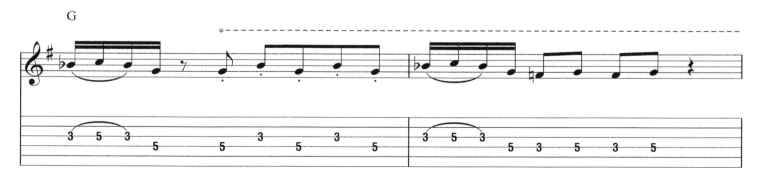

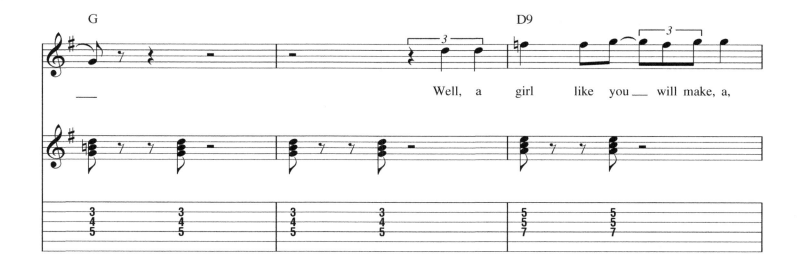

Well, a girl like you __ will make, a,

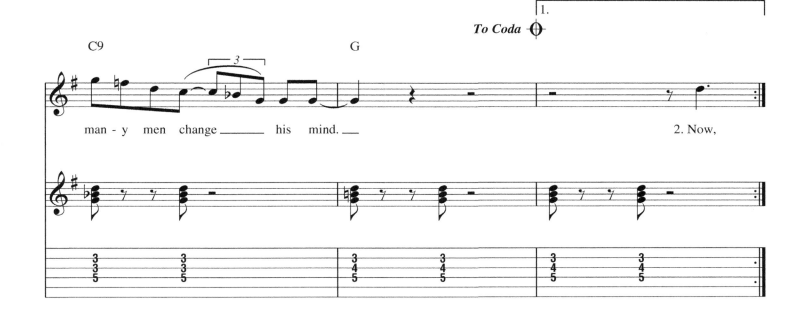

man - y men change _____ his mind. __

2. Now,

3. Let me love __ you, ba - by. _____

Let me

love __ you, ba - by. _____   Whoa, __ let me   love __ you, ba - by.

Yes, __ let me   love __ you, babe. _____   Let me

love   you, ba - by, till your   good love   drives _____ me cra - zy.

Guitar Solo

G

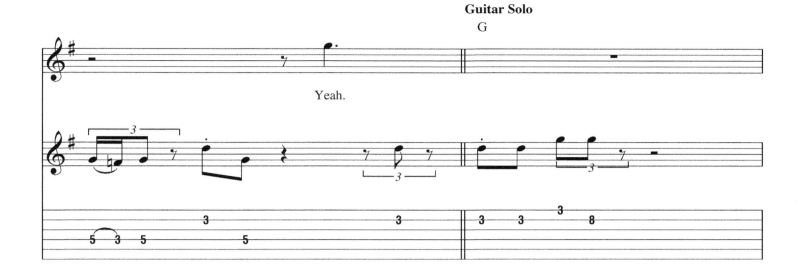

Yeah.

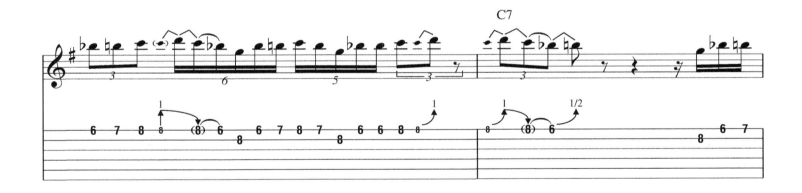

C7

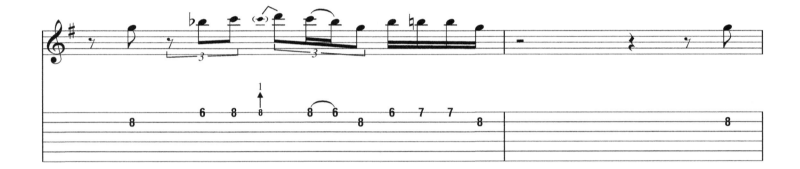

G

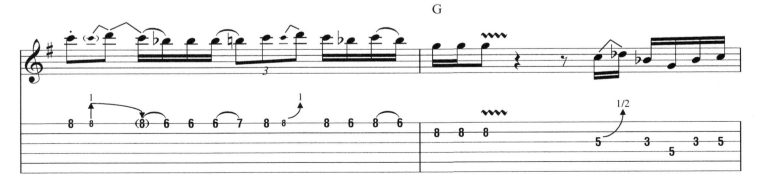

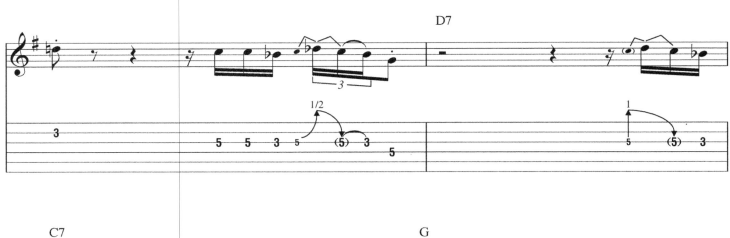

D7

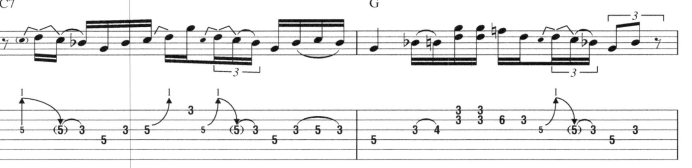

C7

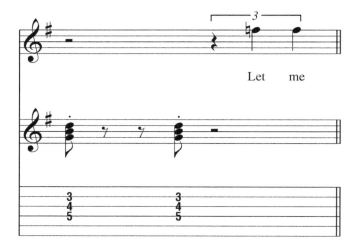

G

D.S. al Coda

Coda

4. I'll ___ give you

Let me

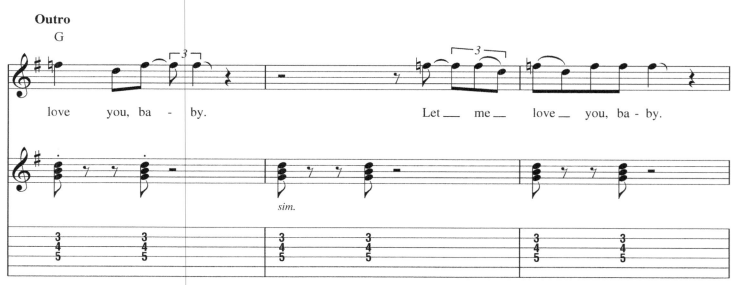

Outro

G

love you, ba - by.

Let __ me __ love __ you, ba - by.

sim.

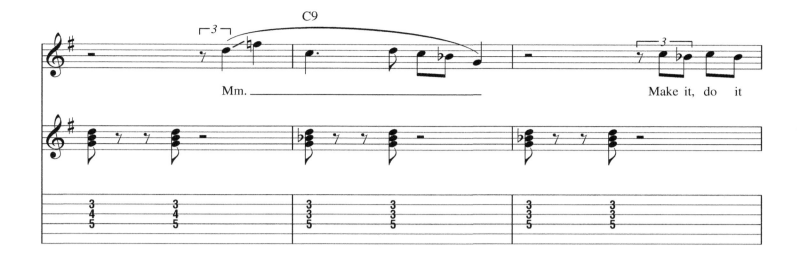

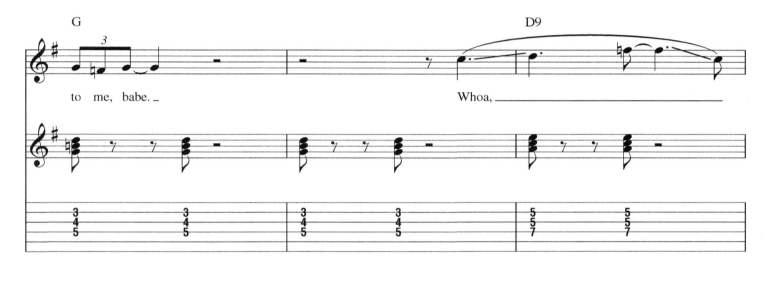

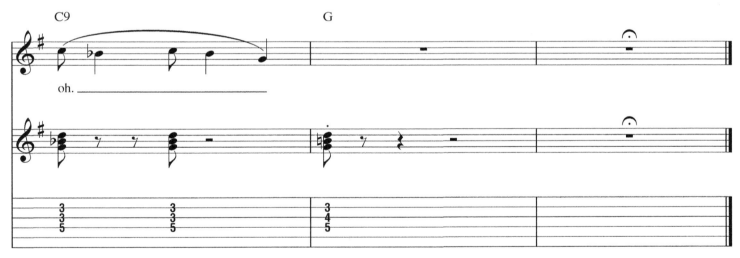

Additional Lyrics

2. Now, baby, when you walk, you know you shake like a willow tree.
   Now, baby, when you walk, you know you shake like a willow tree.
   Well, a girl like you I would love to make a fool of me.

4. I'll give you all I own just for a little bit of your love.
   I'll give you all I own just for a little bit of your love.
   Since I met you, baby, that's all I've been livin' for.

San-Ho-Zay

Words and Music by Freddie King and Sonny Thompson

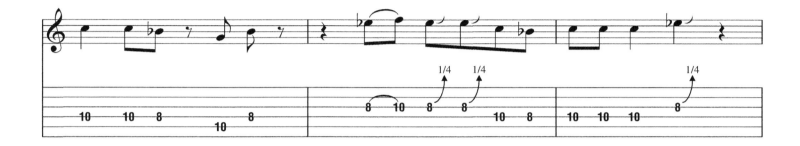

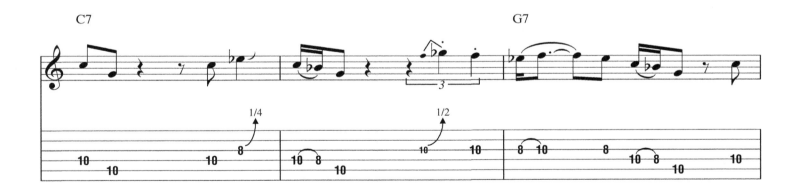

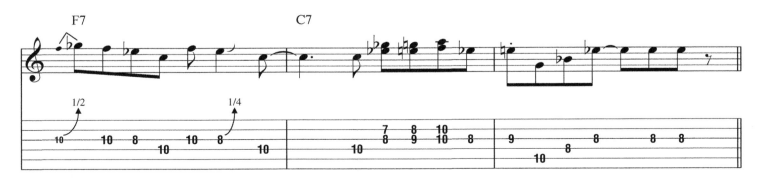

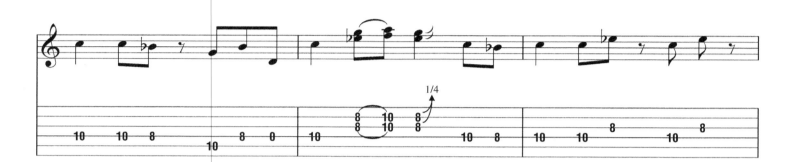

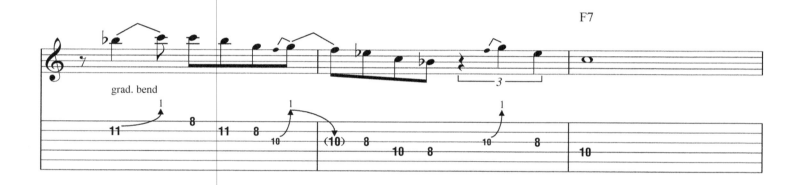

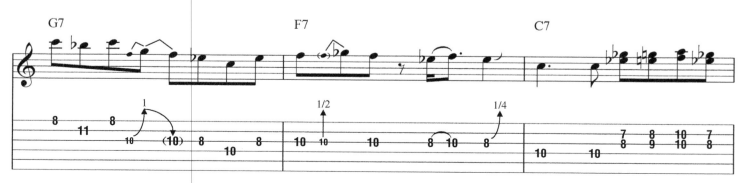

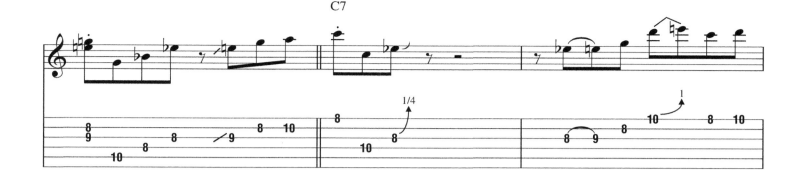

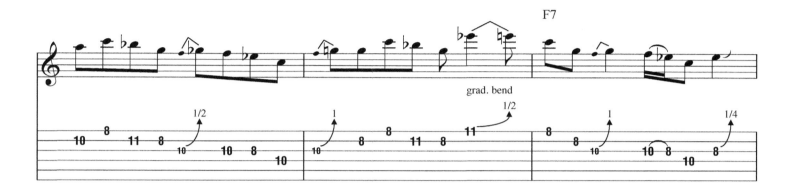

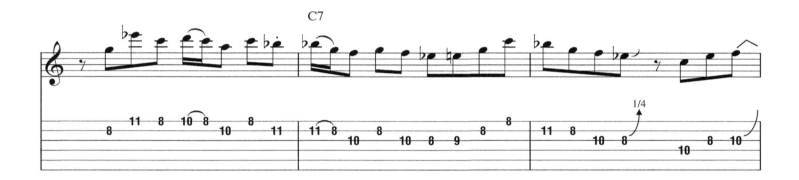

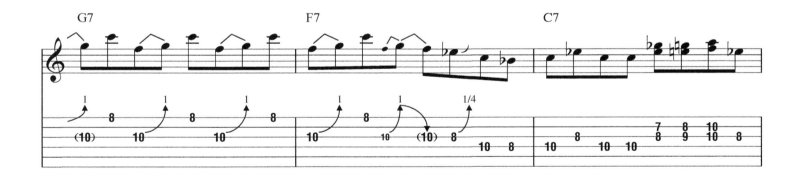

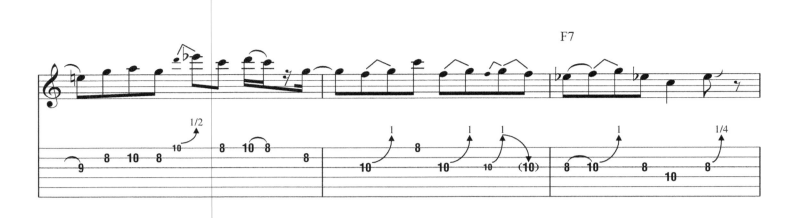

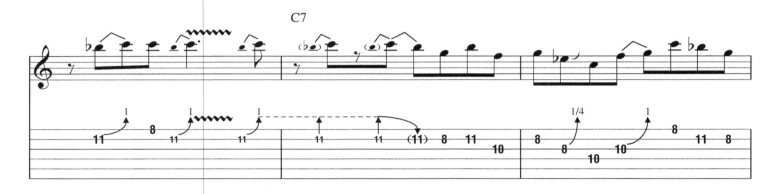

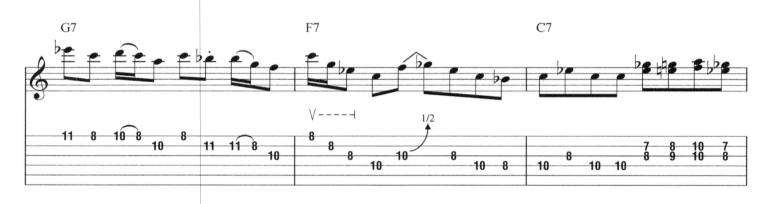

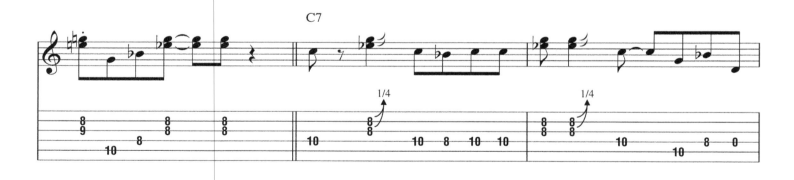

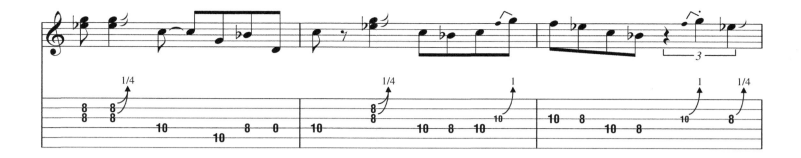

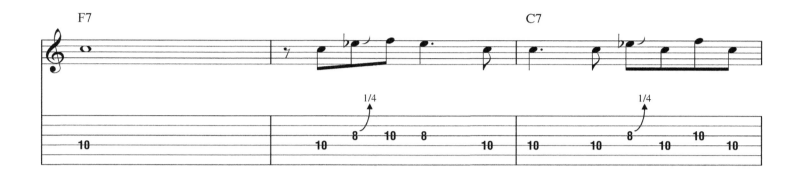

Begin fade

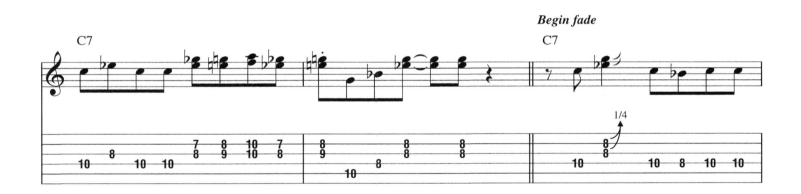

Fade out

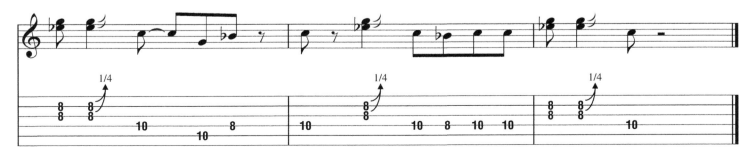

Mary Had a Little Lamb

Written by Buddy Guy

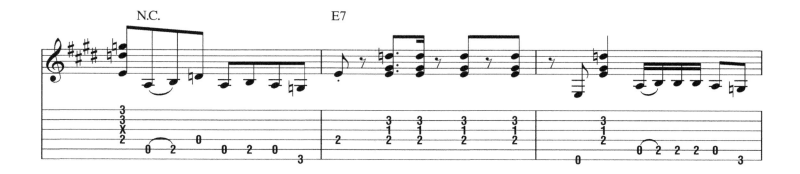

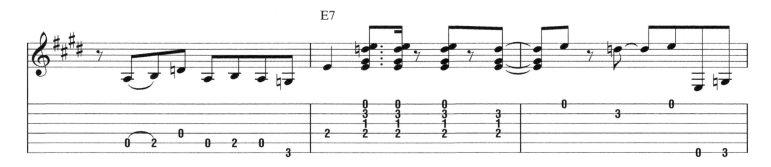

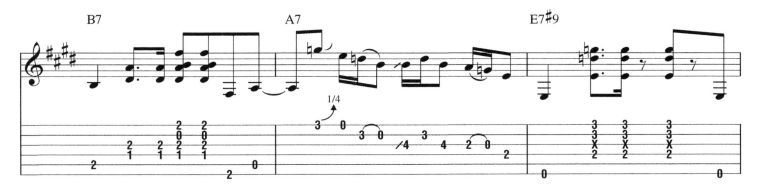

Verse

1. Mar-y had a lit-tle lamb, ___   his fleece was white as   snow,

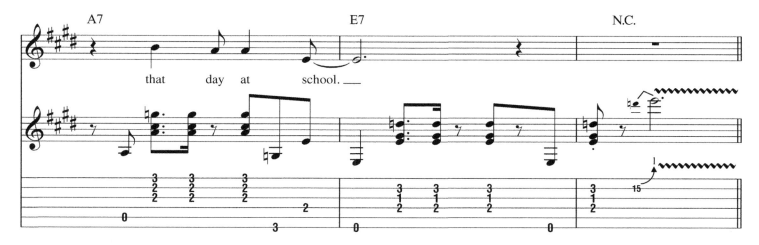

that day at school. ___

Guitar Solo

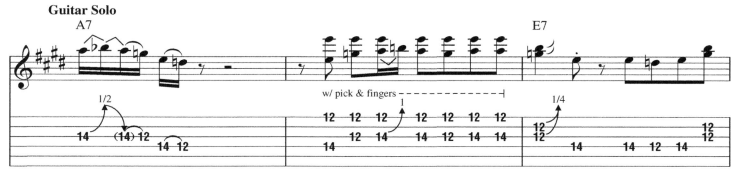

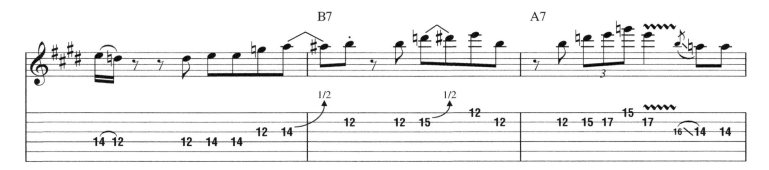

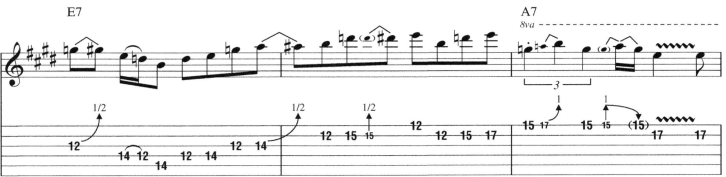

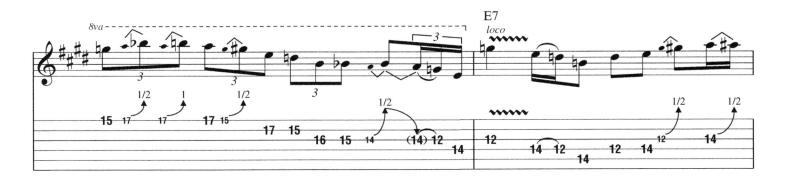

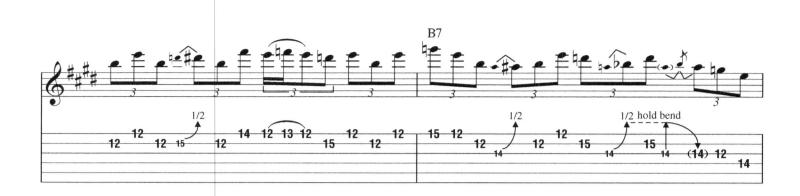

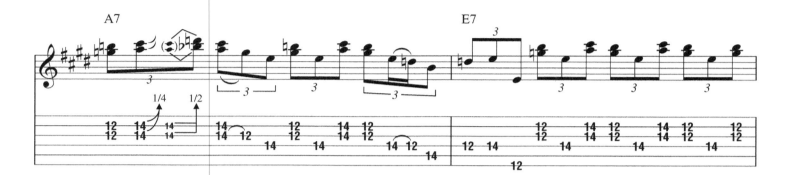

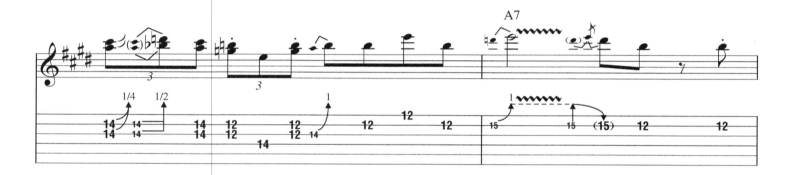

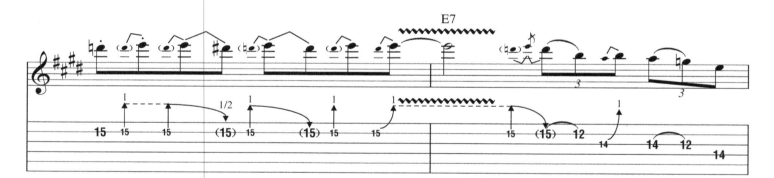

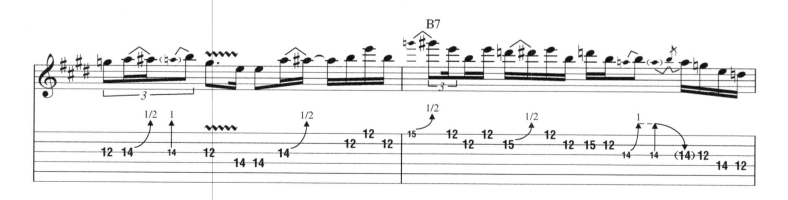

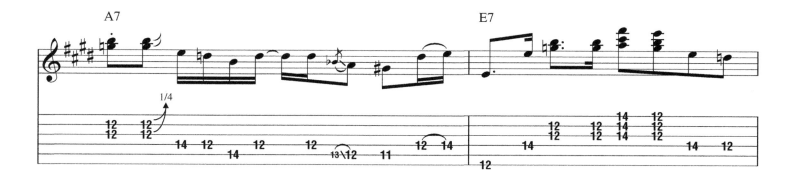

Verse

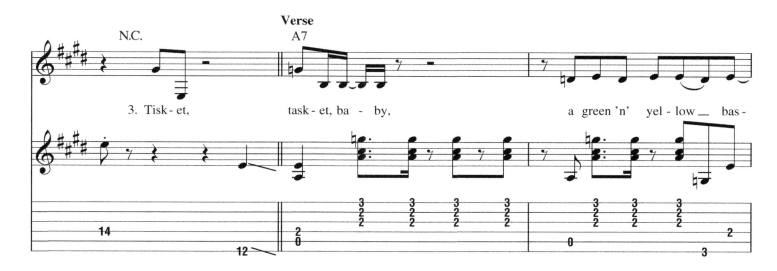

3. Tisk-et, task-et, ba - by, a green 'n' yel-low ___ bas-

- ket. ___ Sent a let-ter to my ba - by, _____

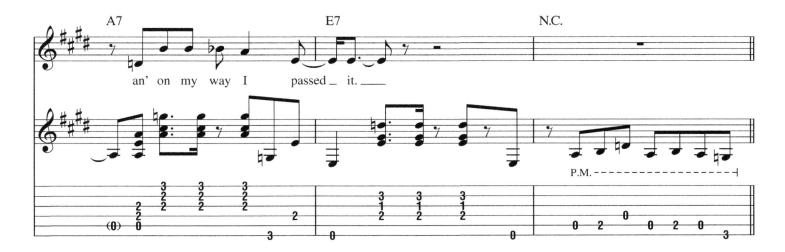

an' on my way I passed ___ it. ____

Outro

T-Bone Shuffle

By T-Bone Walker

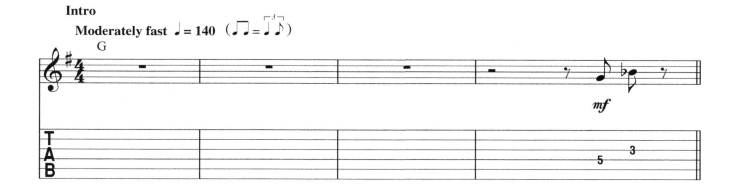

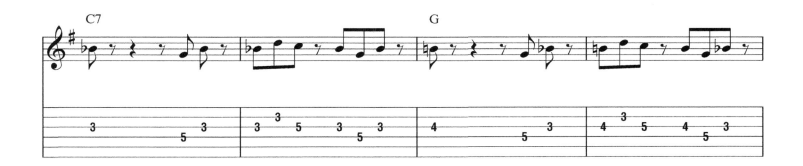

1. Let your hair ___

___ down, ba - by, and let's have ___ a nat - u - ral ball. ___
2., 3. *See additional lyrics*

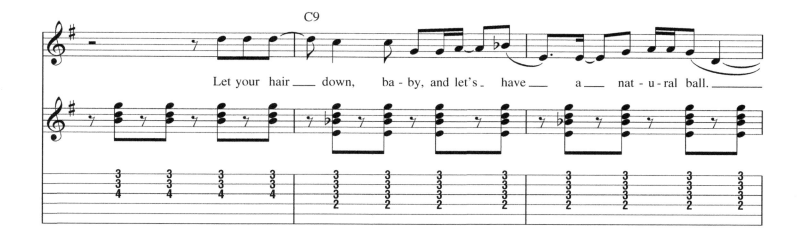

Let your hair down, ba-by, and let's have a nat-u-ral ball.

'Cause when you're not hap-py,

To Coda 2 ⊕ *To Coda 1* ⊕

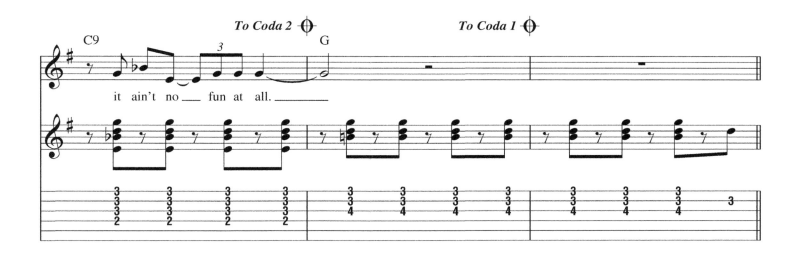

it ain't no fun at all.

Guitar Solo

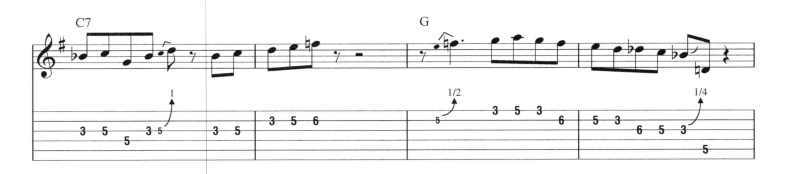

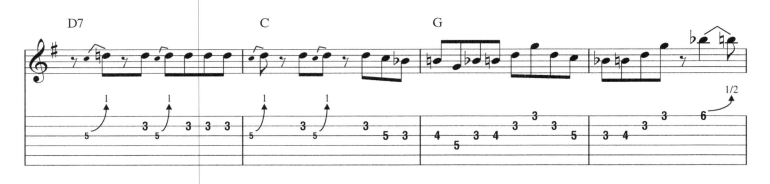

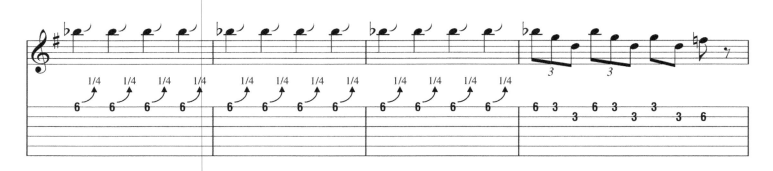

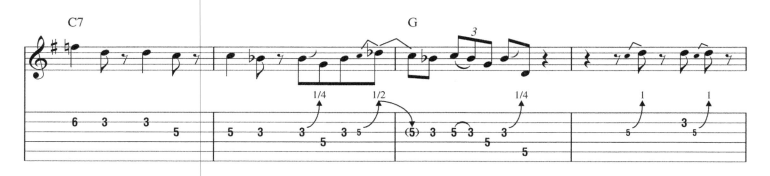

D.S. al Coda 1

2. You can't

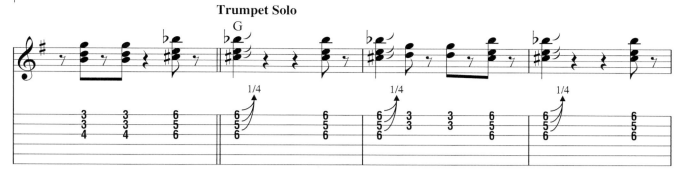

D.S. al Coda 2

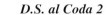

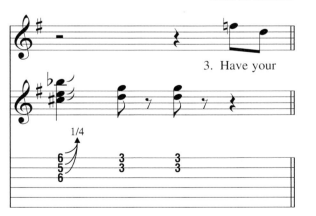

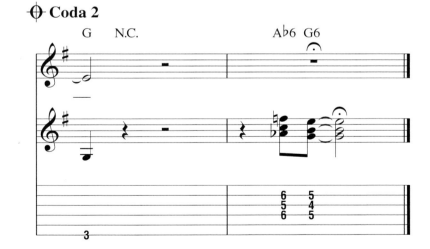

Additional Lyrics

2. You can't take it with you,
   That's one thing for sure.
   You can't take it with you,
   That's one thing for sure.
   There's nothin' wrong with you
   That a good shuffle boogie won't cure.

3. Have your fun while you can, fate's an awful thing.
   Have your fun while you can, fate's an awful thing.
   You can't tell what might happen,
   That's why I love to sing.

GUITAR NOTATION LEGEND

THE MUSICAL STAFF shows pitches and rhythms and is divided by bar lines into measures. Pitches are named after the first seven letters of the alphabet.

TABLATURE graphically represents the guitar fingerboard. Each horizontal line represents a string, and each number represents a fret.

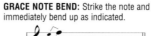

4th string, 2nd fret — 1st & 2nd strings open, played together — open D chord

HALF-STEP BEND: Strike the note and bend up 1/2 step.

WHOLE-STEP BEND: Strike the note and bend up one step.

GRACE NOTE BEND: Strike the note and immediately bend up as indicated.

SLIGHT (MICROTONE) BEND: Strike the note and bend up 1/4 step.

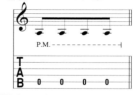

BEND AND RELEASE: Strike the note and bend up as indicated, then release back to the original note. Only the first note is struck.

PRE-BEND: Bend the note as indicated, then strike it.

VIBRATO: The string is vibrated by rapidly bending and releasing the note with the fretting hand.

PALM MUTING: The note is partially muted by the pick hand lightly touching the string(s) just before the bridge.

HAMMER-ON: Strike the first (lower) note with one finger, then sound the higher note (on the same string) with another finger by fretting it without picking.

PULL-OFF: Place both fingers on the notes to be sounded. Strike the first note and without picking, pull the finger off to sound the second (lower) note.

LEGATO SLIDE: Strike the first note and then slide the same fret-hand finger up or down to the second note. The second note is not struck.

SHIFT SLIDE: Same as legato slide, except the second note is struck.

TRILL: Very rapidly alternate between the notes indicated by continuously hammering on and pulling off.

TAPPING: Hammer ("tap") the fret indicated with the pick-hand index or middle finger and pull off to the note fretted by the fret hand.

NATURAL HARMONIC: Strike the note while the fret-hand lightly touches the string directly over the fret indicated.

PINCH HARMONIC: The note is fretted normally and a harmonic is produced by adding the edge of the thumb or the tip of the index finger of the pick hand to the normal pick attack.

TREMOLO PICKING: The note is picked as rapidly and continuously as possible.

VIBRATO BAR DIVE AND RETURN: The pitch of the note or chord is dropped a specified number of steps (in rhythm), then returned to the original pitch.

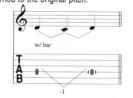

VIBRATO BAR SCOOP: Depress the bar just before striking the note, then quickly release the bar.

VIBRATO BAR DIP: Strike the note and then immediately drop a specified number of steps, then release back to the original pitch.

Additional Musical Definitions

(accent)
- Accentuate note (play it louder).

(staccato)
- Play the note short.

D.S. al Coda
- Go back to the sign (%), then play until the measure marked "***To Coda***," then skip to the section labelled "**Coda**."

D.C. al Fine
- Go back to the beginning of the song and play until the measure marked "***Fine***" (end).

Fill
- Label used to identify a brief melodic figure which is to be inserted into the arrangement.

N.C.
- Harmony is implied.

- Repeat measures between signs.

- When a repeated section has different endings, play the first ending only the first time and the second ending only the second time.